Original title:
The Quest for Meaning: Intermission

Copyright © 2025 Creative Arts Management OÜ
All rights reserved.

Author: Maya Livingston
ISBN HARDBACK: 978-1-80566-272-3
ISBN PAPERBACK: 978-1-80566-567-0

Silhouettes of the Inner World

In the mirror, there's a face,
Wearing socks, yet no shoelace.
Reflecting thoughts, a jumbled mess,
Like trying to solve a Rubik's stress.

My brain's a circus, full of clowns,
Wrapping wisdom in old frowns.
They juggle dreams while I just stare,
Hoping someone else brings the care.

Around the corner, doubts will creep,
Like sneaky squirrels, silent and deep.
They shuffle through each tangled thought,
Playing tricks like friends who forgot.

A treasure chest filled with oddities,
Each shiny piece, a mockery.
Yet somehow in this playful roam,
I find a quirky kind of home.

Between Moments of Silence

In a world where ducks wear hats,
We pause and ponder life's little spats.
Chasing crumbs, or maybe just dust,
In laughter and chaos, we put our trust.

Every giggle is a whispered sigh,
Like a cat that dreams of flying high.
We juggle with thoughts that bounce around,
In the silliness, true wisdom is found.

Echoes of a Lost Journey

There once was a frog who lost his way,
He danced on lily pads all day.
Searching for truth in the ripples so wide,
Finding joy in the slip of a slide.

Each leap was a question, 'What's the plan?'
While chasing shadows, he met a fan.
Together they laughed at the foggy lore,
For meaning, it seems, is a dance on the floor.

Between Shadows and Light

A pigeon with glasses reads the news,
While squirrels debate their next big moves.
Under streetlamps that sing in the night,
We stumble on jokes that bring pure delight.

In the gray, we find hints of red,
Like a clown on a bike with a wobbly head.
Life's strange, like socks that don't belong,
But it's in our quirks, we sing our song.

Threads of Existence

Life's a tapestry stitched with smiles,
And the occasional mix-up of styles.
With each thread pulled, we weave a tale,
Of clowns on tightropes, we never fail.

In the knitting circle, wisdom is spun,
While everyone argues 'who's having fun?'
We wrap ourselves in laughter's embrace,
In the chaos, we find our place.

Between Heartbeats and Dreams

In the chaos of the night, I snore,
My heart dances, while my dreams explore.
A sandwich drifts across the sky,
Peanut butter clouds make time fly.

As I search for meaning, my socks mismatch,
In the realm of dreams, they always catch.
With a giggle and a wiggle, I take flight,
In between the heartbeats, there's pure delight.

Solitude's Silent Symphony

Solo in a room, I groove with a broom,
Whisking dust bunnies away from their gloom.
In tune with the silence, I quirkily croon,
Calling the cat a baffled raccoon.

The walls listen close, they chuckle and sigh,
While I, in a frilly hat, wonder why.
Why the spaghetti weaves tales of its own,
In this symphony of solitude, I'm never alone.

Echoes of a Wandering Mind

Thoughts drift like balloons, off into the blue,
Pondering what flavor of ice cream is true.
A taco stands guard by a fountain of cheese,
While I contemplate life, propelled by a breeze.

In the echoing silence, my brain goes on break,
Chasing after dreams like a runaway cake.
Sipping on ideas brewed strong and wide,
With a fork in my hand, I joyfully slide.

Fragments of Forgotten Time

Somewhere in the attic, nostalgia takes flight,
Dusty old photos reveal the delight.
A dinosaur's birthday, balloons made of pie,
Cousins dressed as superheroes, oh my!

Time tells awkward stories, some stale, some sweet,
A dance party of memories, all on repeat.
As I dig through the rubble, laughter will chime,
In these fragments of life, the silliest rhyme.

Voices in the Void

In a room full of socks, they hold a debate,
Where mismatched pairs ponder their fate.
A lone flip-flop claims it's the best,
While sandals just laugh, feeling blessed.

They argue for hours on colors and styles,
Hoping to find purpose in wire and piles.
But the vacuum cleaner gives a loud sigh,
And the socks all scatter, wishing to fly.

Beyond the Horizon of Understanding

Two spoons sat chatting, full of great dreams,
While forks rolled their eyes, with silent screams.
"We'll sail to the bowl where the soup's so divine,"
Cried one silver spoon, with a glimmering shine.

The forks laughed and tossed bread in their plight,
While spoons imagined a noodle-filled night.
In the drawer, a spatula rolled her eyes,
"You won't find wisdom where pasta resides!"

Whispers of Forgotten Stories

A lost sock whispers stories of feet,
Of glorious journeys and odd, silly feats.
Once a dance partner in a twisty ballet,
Now a lone wanderer, where did it stray?

It dreams of old owners that twirled free,
While dust bunnies giggle, amused as can be.
"The adventure was grand, but now I'm in laundromat limbo,"
It sighs with nostalgia, and still seems to glow.

Nature's Hidden Language

In the garden, the daisies plot and conspire,
While the roses just flaunt, feeling quite higher.
A daisy exclaimed, "Let's speak in the breeze!"
But the roses just laughed, "It's not ours to tease!"

The wind swirled a message of sunshine and rain,
Where thoughts of the lilacs danced free from the pain.
But grass wouldn't budge, feeling too grounded,
Quipped, "The secrets of thorns are best left unbounded!"

Fractured Light

In a world that's turning round,
I tripped on thoughts that made no sound.
Chasing shadows, I lost my shoes,
Find my keys, or just the blues.

Bouncing here, and bumping there,
A jellybean flies through the air.
I laugh at what I couldn't see,
A cosmic joke just out for tea.

Around the bend, I stub a toe,
Imaginary friends, they come and go.
Reflecting on a quirky plight,
Is it wrong if pancakes take flight?

Through fractured light, the answer's near,
Just a wink, and nothing's clear.
I catch a smile, I trip again,
Lost in giggles, I'll try again.

Beneath the Surface of Silence

In whispers soft, the silence hums,
A cocoon where nothing really comes.
Beneath a cloud of sleepy sighs,
A rubber chicken starts to rise.

I search for wisdom in the chat,
But find a joke about a cat.
Conversations stuck in bubble wrap,
Time to unroll, I need a map!

The silence thick as peanut butter,
With chips and guac, it shouldn't flutter.
Yet here I stand, a puzzled gear,
Where's the punchline? Oh, dear, oh dear!

Amid the hush, I chase my thoughts,
But laughter's tangled in the knots.
Beneath the calm, absurdly bright,
I tickle my mind, and it takes flight.

Threads of Connection

I'm weaving tales with gummy bears,
With sprinkles of fun and random flares.
Each thread's an echo, silly, bright,
Can you spot the chaos in the light?

A squirrel pops up, he steals my lunch,
While I ponder if it's all a hunch.
With threads that tangle and knots that bind,
Laughter's the magic that sparks the mind.

As I scribble notes on a pizza box,
I sense the wisdom of the paradox.
Connections thrive on mismatched shoes,
Or maybe it's just my goofy muse.

In quirky patterns, I find my way,
Laughing aloud at the price to pay.
Each thread's a giggle, each stitch a wink,
In the tapestry of thought, I rethink!

Lost in Translation

I shout 'hello!' at an empty chair,
The echo's back, with jokes to share.
In languages that twist and twine,
Are all the gaffes just by design?

A dog barks twice, and then falls flat,
Confused by words, or just a cat?
Translations lost in breakfast toast,
I raise a mug, and laugh the most.

I read the signs in funky fonts,
With every try, my patience haunts.
Trying to ask for a slice of pie,
I end with pizza—oh, my, oh my!

In every fumble, a lesson's found,
In laughter's loop, we spin around.
So here's to words that sometimes crash,
They're the hiccups in life's funny flash.

Resting Between Realities

In a hammock made of thought,
I wonder why I'm always caught.
Is this a dream or just a snack?
I'm munching clouds, where's my snack?

Sipping stars from cups of light,
I check the time, it feels just right.
A giant clown rides by on a cat,
I wave, but he's not time for that.

A whisper from the universe,
In cosmic jokes, I slowly immerse.
Do aliens laugh? I hope they do,
Or maybe they're just taking a snooze.

As nap time rolls, I drift away,
In silly thoughts, I love to play.
When waking up in the same old chair,
I laugh out loud, it's quite unfair!

Dialogues with the Moon

The moon and I share midday tea,
It's strange how she just laughs at me.
I say, 'What's life?' She winks real wide,
'Just chase the cheese and take a ride!'

Her beams tell tales of distant lands,
I spill my drink; she understands.
Together we plot a silly scheme,
To surf on comets and chase a dream.

I ask her why she's pale and bright,
She giggles softly, 'Long, long night!'
I tell her of my daytime blues,
But she just wraps me in silver hues.

We talk of chicken legs and fries,
While plotting stars in the midnight skies.
With laughter shared, I take my leave,
Next time we meet, I'll bring a reprieve!

A Breath on the Edge

Standing at the brink of fate,
I breathe in deep, though it's quite late.
A butterfly flops, showing me how,
To dance on air without a vow.

Yet worries tickle like a bee,
Am I too close to the big, wild sea?
I surely hope the waves don't roll,
Or carry me off, with my silly soul.

A deep breath turns to a big sigh,
Attracts a cloud that floats on by.
It nudges me, 'Hey, come take a ride!'
I say, 'Will there be snacks?' it replied.

With a grin, I leap into flow,
A twist, a turn, a twirl, a glow.
And when I land, all drenched in glee,
I forgot about the edge—just me!

Collisions of Dream and Dust

In the cosmic circus, I'm the jester,
I juggle dreams and fill with luster.
A clumsy star falls at my feet,
"Oops," I say, "That's not very neat."

Dust bunnies scatter with each laugh,
Chasing echoes of the aftermath.
With a whoop and a holler, I bound around,
Making merry in the lost and found.

Time hiccups as I jump and spin,
Floating through whims, I let them in.
"Is my life a riddle or a game?"
I smile and say, "Both sound the same!"

As sleep beckons, I close my eyes,
With giggles swirling 'neath golden skies.
I float in dreams with dust in tow,
In this funny world, where silliness grows!

Where the Shadows Dance

In corners where the dust bunnies play,
A sock puppet dreams of being a chef one day.
He whips up banter, adds a dash of flair,
While shadows giggle in the cozy air.

They waltz through the whispers of secret night,
Believing they're stars, oh what a sight!
With mismatched socks doing the tango too,
Life's little moments, bizarre but true.

The Dance of Uncertainty

Woke up this morning, can't find my shoe,
Pondering life's purpose while I brew some stew.
The fridge hums a tune, oh what a jest,
As I question if I should play or just rest.

Between the curtains, a cat struts with pride,
She knows the answers I try to hide.
Maybe the meaning is in the lost socks,
Or in the rhythm of time's silly clocks.

Timeless Interludes

A squirrel in a hat juggles acorns with glee,
While I sip my coffee, contemplating 'me'.
Time twirls like a dancer, unsure of its stance,
Each moment a chance at a vivid prance.

Snail mail is slow, but the jokes come quick,
Laughter delays the clock, like a clever trick.
In the chaos of seconds, I find little peace,
Yet somehow, it feels like my joy won't cease.

A Tapestry of Moments

Stitching together the days with a thread,
Each laugh and each fumble, there's joy to be fed.
I trip on the lace of my own silly dreams,
Yet float like a poet, or so it seems.

With hiccups and snorts, I navigate time,
Lost in the rhythm, a whimsical rhyme.
These fragments of life, so bright and bizarre,
Weaving a tapestry, a peculiar star.

Reflections in a Shattered Mirror

I gazed at my face, oh what a sight,
Cracks all around me, a fun-house night.
Each piece a riddle, a puzzle to crack,
What's my reflection? I've lost the track.

I smile at the shards, they laugh right back,
Who knew that chaos could follow the hack?
With every odd angle, I chuckle and beam,
Living life's farce, a surreal dream.

A funny man's dance in a fractured frame,
Waving to strangers who feel the same.
I find my humor in tangled threads,
For nothing makes sense in the paths I tread.

So here's to the mirror, all shattered and bright,
A laughter-filled puzzle, what a delight!
Sometimes it's jumbled, however it seems,
Finding my joy in the wildest dreams.

The Space Between Thoughts

In the pause where no thoughts dare to roam,
Sits a potato, claiming it's home.
It shouts, "I'm profound, just not in a bowl!"
And sells tickets to thoughts on a roll.

I wander the silence, what strange delight,
Where giggles of wisdom dance just out of sight.
Ideas like balloons with a mind of their own,
Pop!—I recoil, with laughter I've grown.

A cat with a tie joins the frantic parade,
Reciting old jokes in the bright sunlight's shade.
"Why did the chicken?" I can hear it shout,
But even the chicken has wandered out.

So let's relish the gaps where nonsense can play,
In the space between thoughts, we find our own way.
With silly reflections, we can't go wrong,
Here's to the chaos that keeps us strong!

Journeying Through Stillness

In stillness I tripped over thoughts so deep,
Close call with zen, but I fell fast asleep.
Dreams of a snail dressed in bright, flashy pants,
Who taught me to tango, oh what a dance!

It's quiet, I think—I hear rocks start to snore,
Crickets in tuxedos, what a crafty score!
The trees whisper secrets, they giggle and sway,
Nature's own circus, oh what a display!

I search for the path, but it's hiding in glee,
Pinecones are chuckling, right back at me.
The sun throws confetti, the stars join the fun,
Journeying through stillness? Oh, what a run!

So let's toast to the silence that's waiting in line,
Where laughter echoes in each hidden sign.
As I'm journeying through, I trip and I dive,
Finding joy in the still, oh I feel so alive!

On the Edge of Epiphany

Perched on the brink, my thoughts do a jig,
Like frogs in a pond, all ready to dig.
What's wisdom, you ask, as I scratch my chin?
It's finding your glasses when they're on your skin!

I peek over edges where cliffs call my name,
Popcorn thoughts bubble, bursting with fame.
"I've figured it out!" as I leap with a grin,
But it's only my lunch that tumbled right in.

The universe laughs as I clutch at a clue,
While squirrels take bets on what I will do.
I scribble in circles, trying to see,
Only to find I'm the fool of the spree.

So on the edge where clarity spins,
I'll toast to the madness – it's where life begins!
With wisdom like bubbles that fizz and then pop,
Epiphanies dance, but the giggles won't stop!

Footsteps on Unmarked Paths

I wandered far with mismatched shoes,
Each step I took, I'd then confuse.
The grass, it whispered silly tunes,
As I danced 'neath the laughing moons.

I met a goat who spoke in rhymes,
He shared his thoughts in choppy chimes.
With every word, I lost my way,
But oh, the fun we had that day!

A squirrel joined, with acorn crown,
Claimed he was king of this silly town.
We held a feast of nuts and cheese,
And chuckled loud like summer breeze.

So here I am, with no clear plan,
Just the laughter of a goat and a tan.
In unmarked paths, I find my light,
With every twist, I spark delight.

The Breath Before the Leap

I stood on cliffs, with wings askew,
The ground below said, "Are you true?"
With every breath, my heart raced fast,
I pondered if this fun would last.

A bird nearby sang happy tunes,
It chuckled loud, "Just jump, you goon!"
I took a breath, mouth full of air,
And thought, maybe I don't really care.

With friends below, they waved and cheered,
While I stood back, feeling quite weird.
Then I leaped, embraced the wind,
And landed soft, my laughter pinned.

So here's to leaps from lofty heights,
With friends and giggles, endless sights.
The thrill we chase is wild and deep,
In fun, we leap, in joy, we reap.

Moments of Quiet Revelation

In silence, I once lost my mind,
Searching for treasures I couldn't find.
A cookie jar whispered secrets sweet,
It welcomed me with crumbs and treats.

Amidst the chaos, I wore a hat,
With feathers high, like Cinderella's cat.
I sat and pondered, under a tree,
Wondering what all this meant for me.

A raccoon peeked with a clever grin,
He pointed out the joy within.
Sometimes you laugh, sometimes you sigh,
In quiet moments, we learn to fly.

So here I scribble all my thoughts,
With giggles caught in tangled knots.
In clever whispers, truths unfold,
In goofy paths, our hearts turn gold.

Unraveled Threads

I found some yarn and joyfully spun,
Creating patterns, oh what fun!
But knots appeared, a tangled mess,
My masterpiece turned to a dress!

With every loop, a laugh I'd glean,
My cat, the critic, was quite mean.
He pawed and pounced, knocked down my thread,
Said, "Not all great art is meant to spread."

So we unraveled, side by side,
Chasing each other, full of pride.
With laughter echoing through the hall,
We found our rhythm, embraced the fall.

In tangled ends, we found delight,
With every twist, we sparked the night.
Though threads may fray and patterns blur,
In silly moments, joy will stir.

Between Chaos and Calm

In the whirl of socks and crumbs,
I ponder life, with all its hums.
Should I bake or should I clean?
Decisions made with peanut butter sheen.

A squirrel saunters, glances my way,
What wisdom do you hold today?
Sprinkle laughter, sprinkle cheese,
Focus shifts with playful ease.

In the mix of ups and downs,
Life's a jester in ruffled gowns.
Come along, let's take a stroll,
Navigate this laughable bowl.

So here I sit, amongst the they,
Crumpled thoughts in disarray.
Yet in this merry, wobbly jam,
I find the joy, I find the scam.

Dance of the Unanswered

On a stage of scattered thoughts,
The questions twirl, like tangled knots.
Why does my coffee taste like tea?
Am I the dancer, or the debris?

A cat performs a graceful leap,
Into the air, while I still sleep.
"Are you my muse?" I softly croon,
She blinks at me, then strums a tune.

In the hustle of trivial plight,
I chase my tail—what a delight!
Stars align in the wrong old hat,
Yet here I sway, instead of that.

With twirling minds and crazy glee,
I find the answers, near the brie.
Just pop the cork, let laughter flow,
In questions deep, the fun will grow.

The Kaleidoscope of Essence

A spin of laughter, a twist of fate,
Life's like a game, let's not be late.
With jellybeans and rainbow spritz,
We ponder life in playful fits.

Colors clash, a vivid parade,
Ideas bloom, while worries fade.
Should I wear a tie or a tutu?
Decisions made, with ice cream to pursue.

Amidst the chaos, a smile breaks,
Pondering if the dog speaks in flakes.
Jumping jacks or just a snack?
Life's sweet dance, never a lack.

Spinning circles, the essence flows,
Through giggles, the absurdity grows.
In this chaotic, joyous spree,
The meaning hides behind a tree.

Reverberations of the Mind

Thoughts bounce like a rubber ball,
What's the plan? I can't recall.
Should I wear shoes or cozy socks?
The universe laughs, it certainly rocks.

Pondering on potato chips,
A sandwich takes extensive trips.
As whispers echo, I start to giggle,
In this mental race, just take it simple.

Cats have secrets, dogs are wise,
Do they know what's in the skies?
I greet them in my morning haze,
They glance real back, what a craze!

So let's embrace this light-filled quest,
With wiggles, jiggles, laughter blessed.
For in the end, we find our play,
In reverberations, come what may.

Wading Through Clouds of Thought

I ponder in my fluffy coat,
Swallowed by thoughts like a boat.
Noses twitch in puffy grace,
Lost in a dreamy, bumpy place.

Ideas float like dandelion seeds,
Each one laughs and giggles, it leads.
I chase them 'round an airy maze,
Tripping over my own gaze.

Silly musings parade in line,
Waving banners made of twine.
They fizzle, pop, and sometimes squawk,
In my head, they dance and talk.

But here I stand, in silly plight,
Inclouded thoughts just feel so right.
So pour some coffee, take a leap,
For in this haze, I cheerfully sleep.

In the Limbo of Dreams

Caught between the twinkle and gleam,
I waltz about in a noodle dream.
Flying on marshmallow wings,
Bouncing off the silliest things.

Fish in suits are having tea,
While jellybeans do the cha-cha free.
A cat with glasses reads a book,
And grabs the last worm with a hook.

Tickled by whims that float and glide,
With unicorns right by my side.
The clock is melting, time's a joke,
Both solemn and a little broke.

Yet in this limbo, I find my cheer,
In a world that swirls—I can persevere.
So let's spin around, and never fret,
For laughter is the best duet.

Sketching Reality

With crayons bright, I draw my fate,
In colors bold, I create my state.
Stick figures dance, they trip and fall,
A masterpiece? Oh, not at all!

Reality's a canvas near,
My wild strokes sometimes bring a tear.
Yet in the mess, there's beauty profound,
A giggle here, a snort around.

I dabble in dreams, I sketch a sun,
With chocolate rivers that freely run.
Scribbles of joy that always gleam,
In moments silly as a daydream.

So grab your brush, let laughter flow,
Let absurdity take the show!
Painting smiles amidst the strife,
In a playful, whimsical life.

Pockets of Serenity

I hide my laughter in cozy seams,
In pockets strewn with daydream beams.
Finding peace in pancake stacks,
Where syrup drizzles, and joy cracks.

Each moment's like a friendly cat,
Purring softly in a sunlit flat.
A sprinkle of silliness, a dash of grace,
In the comfort of this happy place.

Life's a circus, with pies on faces,
Yet in the chaos, sweet solace embraces.
Balloons are bouncing, laughter rings,
In pockets snug, where contentment clings.

So stash some giggles for rainy days,
And let your smile light up the ways.
In absurdity's clasp, we twiddle our glee,
Finding serenity in all that's free.

The Intermediary Shadows

In shadows cast by late-night snacks,
I ponder life and write in tracks.
My fridge is full, my mind is bare,
Lost between the dreams and chair.

A cat walks by, a judgmental glare,
While I'm in pajamas, without a care.
The cosmos whispers - 'What's the plan?'
I giggle and hide behind a fan.

For every step my thoughts do flounder,
I find a new snack, my new wonder.
With crumbs of wisdom on my chin,
I ponder all the places I've been.

Yet in this pause, so blissful, free,
I wonder if the world's for me.
So I laugh and dance, my mind a maze,
In shadows where I greet the haze.

Outward Bound

In search of shores where laughter reigns,
I pack my dreams in silly trains.
With rubber ducks and bold balloons,
I chart my path through joyous tunes.

The stars align in goofy ways,
While I navigate through cluttered bays.
I trip on socks, I trip on fate,
And wander off, a little late.

"Oh captain, captain!" I shout in jest,
"Where are we going?" - "Well, a rest!"
With fish that talk and clouds that snore,
We wave at life, then seek for more.

Through all the whirl and silly spin,
I find my joy where chaos begins.
For if the map just laughs and frowns,
I'll sail through storms, and leave the bounds.

Embracing the In-Between

In moments caught 'tween nap and snack,
I find the wisdom I always lack.
The universe hums a lullaby,
While I debate on how to fly.

What if the couch is my chariot?
Or chips the key to being brilliant?
With sip of soda, I ponder fate,
Each bubble bursts, a laugh to date.

I juggle thoughts like apples rare,
And drop them all without a care.
In betwixt the chaos, sweet and weird,
I giggle at what life has steered.

So here I stand, this awkward space,
With pie in hand and whipped cream face.
If life's a jest, a game supreme,
I'll dance between the laugh and dream.

Letters to the Unknown

Dear Unknown, how are you today?
I hope you're munching on dreams and clay.
Do you enjoy the socks left behind?
And wonder what they could find?

I'm sipping tea, just by the bin,
I write to you from inside my skin.
My cat thinks you might be a ghost,
But I'm like, 'You're the one I roast!'

So let's converse in doodles stark,
And draw our thoughts, a wild arc.
With quirky pens and giggling lines,
We'll find the treasures that life defines.

So, dear Unknown, let's not delay,
Send me a joke—brighten my day!
For in this pause, we may just learn,
That laughter is the flame we burn.

In the Midst of Flying Feathers

A chicken crossed the road one day,
In search of wisdom, come what may.
But in a field of clouds, she soared,
Flapping wings where logic's bored.

With ducks debating rows of corn,
She thought instead, of how to yawn.
Notes of laughter filled her beak,
In feathered laughter, truth is weak.

Each egg she'd laid, a feathered quest,
Searching for joy, or simply rest.
But every peck led to a pun,
A fowl affair, and oh what fun!

So from that day, in skies so blue,
She deemed life's riddle, a silly zoo.
Where every flap is just a show,
In the circus of what we don't know.

The Space Between Stars

In the cosmos, where stardust twirls,
A comet sneezes, sending pearls.
Asteroids dance in a waltz so grand,
While aliens juggle with one hand.

Constellations complain of their weight,
Every star's light, a cosmic plate.
They ponder if they're just a joke,
A pun between worlds, a starry folk.

Black holes giggle, swallowing time,
In the void, they ponder a rhyme.
With each blink, more wonders appear,
As galaxies chuckle, "What's the deal here?"

So in this space, where laughter glows,
The universe tickles, as stardust flows.
It whispers soft, a cosmic tease,
Finding joy in the night's cool breeze.

Lost in Thought's Embrace

A squirrel sat under a thinking tree,
Contemplating snacks, who's cleverer, he?
With acorns stacked high as his witty grin,
He pondered if thoughts were just nuts within.

His mind raced like cars on a silly track,
What could he wear, a cap or a sack?
In the ponder of pondering, time flew away,
As birds chirped jokes, and squirrels would play.

Then came a thought, a shimmering star,
"What if life's just a giant bazaar?
Where dreams are the fruits of a candy shop,
And laughter's the currency, never to stop!"

So he danced with ideas, a comical spree,
In that hug of thoughts, he felt truly free.
For in each silly twist, he found a surprise,
A treasure of nonsense within his wise.

Unseen Bridges

Beneath the surface of everyday hues,
Lies a bridge made of laughter, a path of clues.
Where socks take flight, and dust bunnies sing,
On unseen spans, goofy wonders cling.

A bridge of dreams, built with silly string,
Connecting the mundane to fanciful bling.
With shoes on the ceiling and glasses askew,
Who knew that life's whimsy could feel so new?

How do we cross it? With a hop and a skip,
A twirl of the mind, or a finger on lip?
Balancing patience on a rubbery beam,
With laughter as laughter, the ultimate theme.

So if you find joy in places unseen,
Just glide on these bridges, dance in between.
For life's little quirks are its greatest return,
In this circus of life, let curiosity burn.

Lingering at Life's Crossroads

I stood at the fork with a pizza slice,
One path was long and the other precise.
The sign said "Go left and you'll find your way,"
But my gut said right, so I had to stay.

Traffic lights blinked, all colors confused,
I waved at the cars like a dance party schmooze.
Was I the conductor, or just lost in thought?
Either way, a great story that I never sought.

A squirrel stopped by, wearing shades and a hat,
He asked for directions, I said, "How 'bout that?"
Together we pondered, the world so absurd,
And laughter erupted, without a single word.

So here I linger, in silly dismay,
At life's silly crossroads, where I choose to play.
With each twist and turn, let the joy be the guide,
For in this wild jungle, we'll roam side by side.

The Art of Becoming

I woke up one morning, a caterpillar anew,
With dreams of becoming a great butterfly too.
But on my way there, I tripped on a shoe,
And landed in yogurt, oh absurdity's view!

I pondered my fate, can I still fly high?
When a ladybug laughed, as she buzzed by.
"Embrace who you are, in this messy cocoon,"
She winked and then danced, under the bright moon.

"Just don't rush the process, it's part of the game,
Even daisies won't bloom overnight, quite the same."
So I sat in the yogurt, pondering the road,
And made yogurt art while I lightened my load.

With each slip and slide, I learned to enjoy,
Life's art of becoming, it's no simple ploy.
So here's to the mishaps, the stumbles, the falls,
In this grand gallery of life, we'll hang on the walls.

In Search of Lost Colors

Once there was a painter, who lost all his hues,
He searched high and low, for the reds and the blues.
With a brush in his hand, and a frown on his face,
He knocked on the door of the color-filled space.

Spectrum expiring, he needed a fix,
He tried yelling loudly, but got stuck in the mix.
Then a rainbow appeared, with a wink and a grin,
"Just take a deep breath, let the fun times begin!"

They splashed through the puddles, and danced in the sun,
The colors returned, and they laughed on the run.
He learned that the shades were inside him all along,
For even in gray, he could still hum a song.

With every vibrant arc, his worries took flight,
He painted his heart with the joy of pure light.
Now each stroke of his brush tells a story to see,
In a world full of laughter, he found harmony.

Ebb and Flow of Understanding

The waves of my thoughts crashed onto the shore,
Where questions ran wild, wanting answers galore.
A seagull squawked out, "What's the point of it all?"
I shrugged and replied, "Just have fun on the ball!"

As tide pools reflected the skies full of laughs,
I waded in puddles while crafting my drafts.
For wisdom's a puzzle, with pieces awry,
And learning's a game where surprise is the prize.

With each ebb that took something, came a flow in return,
I dug for the shells where the lessons would churn.
Rethinking my stance on the sand of today,
I'd say life is a riddle, let's play it our way!

So here we will gather, in nonsense's embrace,
With giggles and guffaws, we will find our place.
For amidst all the chaos, the splashes, the fun,
Understanding is weird, but joy's never done!

Pages Unwritten

In the library of dreams we roam,
Papers scattered, no need for home.
A cat with glasses reads aloud,
While we dance like clowns, feeling proud.

With quills like swords, we duel the blank,
A witty bird gives us a prank.
Words fly past like crazy bees,
In this madness, we find our ease.

Each scribble a tale of slips and trips,
Between coffee sips and funny quips.
We trip on thoughts, and giggle too,
In a world where silliness feels brand new.

So come along, let's write our play,
Where nonsense paves a wacky way.
A chapter closed, but laughter stays,
In pages unwritten, our hearts will blaze.

In Search of First Light

At dawn, we trip over sleeping dreams,
Chasing shadows and silly schemes.
The sun yawns wide, a giant cat,
While we spin circles, 'What's up with that?'

With coffee cups as our shiny shields,
We roam the fields where nonsense yields.
Ducklings follow, they quack in delight,
As we frolic toward the morning light.

With maps drawn in crayon, we head across,
A treasure hunt for giggles, never loss.
We stumble on riddles left by the day,
In every silly turn, we laugh and play.

So here we are, a motley crew,
In search of the light that feels so new.
With joy in our hearts and laughs on repeat,
We greet each sunrise, absurd and sweet.

A Pause for Contemplation

In the garden of thoughts, we take a seat,
Where daisies gossip and sunflowers greet.
A ponderous snail takes its leisurely walk,
While we chuckle at clouds that seem to talk.

With pickle-flavored wisdom in hand,
We decipher the meaning that's scattered like sand.
A butterfly whispers, 'It's all just a show,'
And we laugh at the wisdom we thought we would know.

We sip from the cup of absurdity's brew,
Contemplating life with a playful view.
A frog in a suit leaps into the fray,
Exclaiming, 'Why not? Let's dance the day away!'

So let's pause in this whimsical song,
Finding joy in where we belong.
In wonders strange, let our hearts just sway,
In this pause for thought, let laughter play!

The Map of Uncertainty

With a map made of riddles and a compass of cheer,
We wander the paths where the laughter is clear.
A squirrel in a hat gives directions, so bold,
While giggles are currency, worth more than gold.

Where arrows point sideways and skies turn bright,
We find our way through a whimsical night.
Navigating nonsense with style and flair,
Every wrong turn leads to fun—we don't care!

In a forest of giggles, we seek out the sound,
Of laughter that echoes and joy all around.
With each twist and turn, we stumble and glide,
On this map of uncertainty, it's fun to abide.

So hold out your compass, let's dance in the rain,
In this zany adventure, we'll never feel pain.
For in the unknown, with humor as guide,
We plot our own course on this laugh-filled ride.

The Unfolding Pause

In the middle of the thinking game,
I lost my train, it went off-frame.
Searching for sense in a sock drawer,
Found just a sandwich, who needs more?

Time stands still, like a frozen frog,
We ponder truths like an old, wet dog.
Staring at clouds, we might see shapes,
Or maybe it's just a bunch of grapes.

With laughter echoing through the maze,
Life's a circus, in many ways.
Juggling thoughts like clowns on parade,
The ringmaster holds a confused charade.

When the clock ticks funny and starts to play,
We slip on meanings that drift away.
Like socks in the dryer, or time in a race,
We chase the absurd, and find our place.

Navigating the Invisible

Navigating fog with a blindfolded guide,
We trip on questions, go for a slide.
Invisible paths twist under our feet,
Oh look, there's a taco stand, what a treat!

Wandering lost in a brainy bazaar,
Where wisdom is sold from a pushcart car.
I bought a thought, but it came with a catch,
It's stuck in my mind, not a perfect match.

Birds tweet secrets, if we just could hear,
But they sing off-key; it's a bit unclear.
"Follow your heart!" they cheer from the trees,
But mine wants pizza, "Listen to me, please!"

In the end, we may laugh at our plight,
As we navigate nothing like it's a flight.
With maps upside down and compasses wrong,
We waddle through life, still humming our song.

Wanderlust of the Heart

My heart's a wanderer, but it lost its map,
Roaming through candy stores, what a mishap!
Chasing after feelings like escapee balloons,
Only to find them tangled in cartoons.

It wants to dance on the rooftops at night,
But trips on the wire and gives me a fright.
"Chase your dreams!" folks cry, holding their lattes,
While I chase my socks, they peek out of hot bates.

So we hike through the chaos with giggles and glee,
Armored in pizza, as brave as can be.
Love's a riddle, tossed in a box,
Trying to solve it while wearing silly socks.

We laugh through the efforts, that sweet, awkward strife,
In pursuit of the unseen, in the joy of this life.
Every fumbled step, a waltz on the scene,
A comedic ballet, where we all convene.

Fragments of Understanding

I gathered fragments, like shards of a joke,
Peeking through puzzles made from a croak.
Each missing piece a tickle or tease,
As I try to fit them with crumbly cheese.

In the land of confusion, I met a wise fool,
He taught me that logic swims in a pool.
Hiccups of wisdom, who knew they could sound,
Like a rubber chicken dropped on the ground?

Searching for answers in a cereal bowl,
There's a prize inside, but it's taken its toll.
Sugar-coated truths, like sprinkles on cake,
Dissolve in the milk, how much can I take?

Through giggles and grumbles, we find our way back,
To laughter and love, with joy in the slack.
So here's to the moments we pick up the phones,
To share in the madness of quirky old bones.

Chasing moments of Clarity

In a world of jumbled thoughts,
I lost my keys, can't find my socks.
I chase the wisdom like a cat,
But it hides beneath my cluttered rocks.

I ponder deep while eating pie,
The flavor brings me close to grace.
Yet crumbs litter my shirt and tie,
It's hard to think while crumbs embrace.

I asked a squirrel to share his wit,
He chattered back, a cryptic tease.
Between the nuts and little skits,
I wonder if I'm doomed to freeze.

But laughter whispers in the night,
And joy may not be far away.
I'll keep on dancing in the light,
If only for a silly play.

Reflection Over Water

By the pond, I see my face,
A duck swims by, he laughs with glee.
"Is this my life?" I ponder, brace,
He quacks, "Too deep, just be like me!"

I toss a stone, it splashes high,
The ripples laugh, they twirl and twist.
"Is wisdom found in a simple pie?"
The duck just quacks, "You've got a list."

Mirrors of water, secrets flair,
I sip the thoughts like it's a drink.
But ducks and fish they just don't care,
While I'm still stuck in mind's deep sink.

In muddled waves, I find a spark,
Life's silly dance holds no true plan.
With every splash, a joyful lark,
I float on dreams, a happy man.

Nature's Unfolding Story

A tree stood still, with arms outstretched,
It whispered tales of days gone by.
I asked it secrets, though it fetched,
A squirrel stole my nuts nearby.

The flowers laughed as they did bloom,
"We don't have time to waste on you."
I pondered life, amidst this room,
Of buzzing bees and skies of blue.

In every petal, stories thrive,
As critters scoot in rhythmic glee.
Though I'm still here, unsure, deprived,
Nature chuckles, "Just wait and see."

Tickling winds brought me a breeze,
An invisible giggle takes flight.
Perhaps the chaos is a tease,
Laughing me home, both day and night.

Balancing on a Tightrope

Perched above the world so high,
I wobble, juggle thoughts galore.
A clumsy dance, I laugh, oh my!
Who knew this quest would lead to more?

Each step I take, the ground does sway,
I shout, "Is life a circus act?"
The audience throws popcorn my way,
And I reply, "Hey, that's a fact!"

A trampoline bounces back my woes,
With every bounce, I float and fly.
But here's the truth that softly grows:
The tightrope gleefully tells me why.

Balance is found in jests and cheer,
Amid high stakes and laughter's song.
So watch me dance, overcome the fear,
For this madcap life can't be wrong!

Notes from a Silent Mind

In a world of jumbled thoughts,
I tripped over my own brain,
Like a cat upon its paws,
The chase is rather insane.

Pencils scribble, coffee spills,
My planner thinks it's fun,
To dance between the meetings,
While I'm still on the run.

A to-do can wait, I say,
As I grab another snack,
The meaning hides in chocolate,
With no intent to track.

So here's a note from silence,
Where laughs blend with the muse,
In this quirky little circus,
It's my joy I choose to lose.

Amidst the Fading Echoes

Wandering through the hall of echoes,
I found my missing sock,
In conversations with my slippers,
They always talk and mock.

The clock is ticking loudly now,
But only I can hear,
It's playing hide and seek with time,
And I'm the laughing deer.

I asked a shadow for advice,
It shrugged and looked away,
So I danced with fading whispers,
Until the light turned gray.

Oh, the meaning is elusive,
And that's quite the charade,
But who needs profound wisdom,
When you're rocking in your spade!

Thresholds of Discovery

I tiptoe to the door of thought,
Peering through the cracked frame,
It's a carnival of ideas,
That's never quite the same.

Riddles fly like butterflies,
Winging high with silly tunes,
I chase one down a rabbit hole,
While humming to the moons.

Each threshold I have opened wide,
Reveals a wobbly chair,
Where ponderings come to nap,
And I'm the clown in there.

So here's to goofy musings,
Like pies that float and drop,
In this whimsical existence,
I'm the cream on top!

Capturing Fleeting Whispers

In the garden of my wonder,
Whispers swirl like leaves,
I capture them in a jar,
But they just giggle and tease.

A fish asked me for secrets,
As it swam through my bare feet,
"Do frogs know more than us?" it said,
I laughed and offered a treat.

The butterflies debated fate,
Over nectar and sunshine,
I scribble down their banter,
Between my sips of brine.

So if you want true wisdom,
Just listen to the fun,
The meaning's in the nonsense,
Three cheers for the undone!

Unraveled Dreams

In a laundry basket full of socks,
The universe hides inside paradox.
Lost in the shuffle of daily flights,
I miss my chance to uncover insights.

Sailing on thoughts like paper boats,
Wondering why time always gloats.
Chasing shadows in the midday sun,
We laugh as we realize we've just begun.

Tickling fate with a feather's touch,
Every wrong turn doesn't hurt as much.
Life's a circus with clowns galore,
We juggle doubts, and still ask for more.

At the end of it all, we'll sip our tea,
And ponder how silly it all seems to be.
With mismatched shoes and laughter loud,
We take a bow, feeling joyfully proud.

Chasing the Breath of Time

Clock hands spin like a dizzy dance,
Each tick and tock, a fleeting chance.
Racing clouds as they drift and tease,
I chase my breath with sneezes of ease.

Candy floss skies, sugar-coated dreams,
I trip on the pavement, bursting at the seams.
Tickling seconds in playful jest,
Finding joy in this wandering quest.

As breadcrumbs scatter along my path,
I giggle at fortune's silly math.
Adding laughter to the cup of fate,
Oh, why let worries set the date?

With a wink to the stars, I spin around,
In the grand comedy where joy is found.
I pen my script with hiccups and rhymes,
A toast to the chase of life's silly climbs.

Interludes of Reflection

In a mirror cracked, the truth is skewed,
Laughter echoes where worries brewed.
Dancing shadows whisper of dreams,
In between giggles, life's not what it seems.

Searching for answers painted in hues,
In the garden of thought, I prune out the blues.
Planting seeds of whimsy, they bloom and sway,
Brighten the corners where daylight plays.

Mixing solutions in a gumdrop storm,
I ponder the puzzle in its odd form.
Why is sanity always on the run?
Is it hiding in laughter, or is that just fun?

Count the moments like candles that burn,
Laughter's the lesson; it's now my turn.
With each chuckle, I"ll lighten the load,
Reflecting on life as I follow the road.

Seeking the Unseen

With eyes wide shut, I wander the dark,
Hunting for reasons, ready to spark.
Invisible truths dancing like flames,
I trip on the laughter that life loudly claims.

Petting the shadows that flicker and tease,
I scare off the doubts with a resonant sneeze.
Frolicking ghosts play tag with the past,
Sweeping confessions under the cast.

The whispers of wisdom blend with my wine,
Each sip a riddle, each gulp a sign.
Serenade me, oh cosmic jesters, please,
In this theater of life, I'll find my keys.

As curtains fall on the grand charade,
I giggle at journeys, we aren't afraid.
For seeking the unseen is a game divine,
And I'm the player with whimsical shine.

A Breath of Cosmic Air

In a galaxy far, far away,
Aliens sip tea, only to say,
'What's the fuss with Earthlings' plight?
We'd rather dance under the moonlight!'

Stars winkle like silly eyes,
While comets zoom, to our surprise.
They leave behind trails of glittery cheer,
And we forget why we're all here.

Little green men with a curious stare,
Ask, 'Life is heavy, do you need a spare?'
With interstellar jokes and laughter shared,
Who knew the cosmos also cared?

So let's float through space, grab a snack,
And giggle at thoughts we can't hold back.
For amidst the chaos and the flare,
There's joy in just taking a cosmic air.

Chasing Fleeting Truth

Under the sun, truth wears a hat,
It jumps and skips, like a playful cat.
Chasing shadows, we run in vain,
It's a game of hide and seek—what a pain!

The wise old sage sits with a grin,
'Truth is a noodle, let the fun begin!'
So we twirl and tumble down the track,
Bumping into thoughts, we never get back.

With questions like confetti in the air,
We toss them high without a care.
Half the time, we laugh in the dark,
While the other half chases that elusive spark.

But isn't it silly, this endless chase?
Perhaps the truth likes a good hiding place!
We'll giggle and giggle, there's nothing to rue,
Since the journey is richer than catching it too.

In the Stillness of Time

Clock hands tick like a tune out of key,
We sit and wonder, 'What will it be?'
Time has whispers, secrets galore,
But when we ask, it just shuts the door.

In the silence, we munch on some snacks,
Debating the meaning of our missing tracks.
Tick-tock, the moments slip through our fingers,
And the pudding of time just awkwardly lingers.

We spin in circles, like toys that are wound,
Searching for answers, yet none can be found.
With chuckles and sighs, we sip on our tea,
While time shakes its head; 'You'll never catch me!'

So we dance in the stillness, a quirky ballet,
Embracing the silence, come what may.
In the end, let laughter be our chime,
As we float in the fluffy clouds of time.

Waiting for Dawn

The sun takes its time, or so it seems,
While honest to goodness, we count our dreams.
With coffee in hand, we tap our toes,
As the moon winks at us with a knowing pose.

Foggy ideas swirl like morning mist,
Did we forget something? It's hard to persist.
With each minute, our patience grows thin,
'Is today the day that we finally begin?'

Birds chirp loudly, 'Wake up, sleepyhead!'
Yet here we lounge, lost in our bed.
We ponder the wonders of life's bright dawn,
And laugh at the chaos of yesteryear's yawn.

But when the first light starts shining bright,
We'll frolic with joy, oh what a delight!
For in the waiting, we find our own tune,
Eagerly dancing to the dawn's joyful croon.

A Chronicle of Questions

Why do socks disappear, oh dear?
Is it the laundry's sneaky cheer?
Are they plotting a great escape?
In a land of fabric and tape?

Do fish ever hear the sound?
Of their thoughts as they swim around?
Or do bubbles steal their dreams late?
Float away on a watery fate?

Can trees really talk when we're gone?
Sharing secrets with the dawn?
While squirrels plot their next grand heist,
Lurking just behind the slice of yeast?

So many questions, a curious spree,
Life's a riddle—a puzzle for thee.
Yet laughter dances in fragile light,
As we ponder the wrongs and rights.

Minimalist Musings

In a world that's just too vast,
What's the point of running fast?
Is speed just a fancy illusion?
Or a silent, thrilling confusion?

A crumb on the floor means snack time,
Is that a crime or just pure rhyme?
Why do cats sit upon our heads?
Is it their way of picking threads?

A pen in hand, I jotted so,
But what comes next? I do not know.
Will coffee spill redefine my fate?
With every sip, is love too late?

Just thoughts that float like clouds in blue,
A puzzle made of me and you.
But if I laugh while I forget,
Does that make life a little less set?

Crest of Enigma

On the edge of the shore I stand,
Searching for answers in the sand.
What if the waves just want to dance?
Or is it about lost romance?

Wherein lies the key to true delight?
Is it hidden in mischief's light?
Why do daisies always get tall?
And why do I trip, then always fall?

Do rocks have feelings they don't share?
Is that why they sit without a care?
And clouds, do they giggle, float, and play?
While we rush about in the fray?

In riddles and rhymes, life spins around,
Searching for treasures just to be found.
But amid the laughter and silly quirks,
Wit is the treasure as reality lurks.

Uncharted Waters of the Soul

In the ocean's heart, do fish feel bold?
Or is it just a tale that's old?
Can jellyfish play peek-a-boo?
With secrets hidden in the blue?

If snails can race with such slow grace,
Who's the referee in this mad chase?
And why do they carry their homes tight?
Is it comfort found in the night?

What's the recipe for a good cheer?
What spices do laughter hold dear?
Can umbrellas dance and sing a tune?
With a rhythm akin to the moon?

So let's set sail in this journey deep,
Where questions swirl, and answers sleep.
With humor as our guiding star,
We'll sail through life, wherever we are.

Searching Shadows

In the corners, shadows dance,
They slip and slide, not giving chance.
I trip on thoughts, then lose my shoe,
While pondering why the sky is blue.

The broomstick rides, but not quite right,
It creaks and groans beneath the night.
A shadow giggles, I pause and stare,
Does it know more? It's such a scare!

A cat meows, a dog replies,
With secret giggles of their own wise.
Do squirrels plot 'neath the leafy shade?
Or simply play at charades, unafraid?

So I dance with shadows, my quirky friends,
In hilarious chaos, my search never ends.
For meaning's a riddle, or so I conclude,
With laughter's sweet echo, I'm never too rude.

Between Echoes of Silence

In the hush, I slip and slide,
Between whispers, I seek to bide.
The clock ticks loud, but no one's here,
Why does silence feel like cheer?

Echoes play hide and seek with time,
As I try to make my thoughts rhyme.
Is that a yawn or just my brain?
Perhaps a squirrel in search of grain?

The walls have ears, but they don't talk,
They only watch my awkward walk.
I laugh at shadows, they laugh back too,
Both confused by what I should pursue.

So I dance in silence, curiously bold,
Trading stories that never get told.
And here I find my random jest,
Between echoes, I take a rest.

Pause in the Labyrinth

Through winding paths, I stroll and spin,
A puzzle wrapped in a riddle's grin.
Which way is up? I cannot tell,
The walls are giggling, casting a spell.

A minotaur sings, or so I dream,
With dulcet tones of ice cream.
I stop and ponder, ice cream for real?
Or just my mind's odd meal appeal?

I trip on thoughts, the ground's a friend,
In this maze where surprises blend.
Follow the laughter, it knows the way,
Or at least it leads to ice cream buffet!

So I take a pause, with joy in my chest,
In this labyrinth, I find my jest.
With silliness swirling, I break through the haze,
Finding meaning in my own quirky maze.

Reflections on Empty Days

A mirror shows me, but I just grin,
What's in my head? Where to begin?
Reflections of nothing, or maybe a cat,
Who seems to think I'm quite the brat.

Days unfold like origami clowns,
Twisting and turning with silly frowns.
I sip my coffee, it sips me back,
In this swirl of humor, I feel no lack.

Lost in the shuffle, where does it lead?
To selfies with squirrels, that's all I need!
With each laugh echoing, I start to see,
Empty days bloom with absurdity.

So here's to the moments of joyless days,
That turn into laughter, in peculiar ways.
With reflections amused, I dance in the sun,
Finding the fun means life's just begun.

www.ingramcontent.com/pod-product-compliance
Lightning Source LLC
Chambersburg PA
CBHW072143200426
43209CB00051B/333